My Invisible World

Life with my brother, his disability and his service dog

By Morasha R. Winokur

Better Endings New Beginnings
Minneapolis, MN

My Invisible World

Life with my brother, his disability and his service dog

Copyright © 2009 (Revised 2012)

Morasha R. Winokur

Published by:

Better Endings New Beginnings

www.betterendings.org

If you purchase this book without a cover you should be aware that this book may be stolen property and reported as "unsold or destroyed" to the publisher. In such case, neither the author nor the publisher has received any payment for this stripped book.

All Rights Reserved. Except as permitted under U.S. Copyright Act of 1976, no part of this publication may be reproduced, stored in a retrieval system, or transmitted by any means - electronic, mechanical, photocopying, recording or otherwise - without written permission from the publisher.

Reprinted by CreateSpace

ISBN-13: 978-1469903491 ISBN-10: 1469903490

Original ISBN 978-0-9842007-0-2

Library of Congress Control Number 2009934382

In memory of

my Grandma
Sarah "Giggy" Kanter

and my Aunt
Joyce Kanter

This book is dedicated to my brother, Iyal Navon Winokur

Acknowledgements

My family

My parents, Donnie and Harvey Winokur

My Pop-pop, Herb Kanter

My Uncle, Jed Kanter

My Grandma, Meemie (Miriam)

and Papa Doug Winokur

My Aunts, Ilene Alzaid and Randy Ahmed

My cousins, Nadia, Joe, Haya, Meshari and Barrak

All my friends

My past and present teachers

And Chancer's friends

Karen Shirk, Director of 4 Paws for Ability,

Jeremy Dulebohn, and Jennifer Varick,

who helped to train Chancer at 4 Paws

The women at Laken Correctional Center

who also helped train Chancer

And my book crew –

Melissa Laquement; Joel Whisenant; Adair Kanter;

Billie Kanter; Judy Vorfeld; Shelly Glazer;

and especially Jodee Kulp and Liz Kulp

without whom I could not have written this book

Table of Contents

Preface

Chapter 1 - M.F.B

Chapter 2 - A Sad Discovery

Chapter 3 - Our Family

Chapter 4 - Life Longggg

Chapter 5 - Grand Slam or Shut Out

Chapter 6 - Second Chances

Chapter 7 - "Talk to the Paw"

Chapter 8 - Jumping in With Four Paws

Chapter 9 - The un-Amusement Park

Chapter 10 - I Love My Mom, but...

Chapter 11 - Out and About

Chapter 12 - Visible New Paw Prints

Glossary

Morasha's Scrapbook

Blankies for Babies

Preface

Hi My name is **Morasha** and in Hebrew my name means 'legacy'. My middle name is **Rael**, which means 'guardian'. I am not sure I like the name Rael or its meaning because being a guardian is a hard job and soon you will understand why.

I'm the assistant dog handler in our home. My job is to help my mom with Chancer, our service dog, in dog handling commands. We haven't always had a service dog in our home, but we've needed one.

My life began in Russia, a long way from the United States. That seems like a lifetime ago. My "baby babble" Russian is now English and I consider English my main language.

Iyal, my brother, and I came to this country through adoption. We were both born in Astrakhan, Russia, a little over eleven years ago. My name then was 'Olga', (pronounced Ol-ya). In Russian it means 'Holy', but in English it sure sounds like Oreo to me!

I laughed with joy when my new Mom and Dad arrived to greet me for the first time. Mom and Dad took videos of our meeting and I still like watching those videos from that place so very far away and long ago.

My brother, Iyal, was not so lucky. We did not live in the same Children's House in Astrakhan. Mom and Dad met 'Andrey' who became **Iyal Navon Winokur**, in another Children's House. Unlike me, he stayed in his own little world to feel safe and comfortable. His birth name meant 'manly or brave', and he had to be very brave as a baby and rely on himself.

Iyal was given family names after grandfathers and uncles in our new family.

Iyal means '**strength**' or '**deer**' and
Navon means '**wisdom**'.

Iyal's disability made our family become very strong.
My mom's research made our family become wise.

In the beginning Mom and Dad were not worried about his chicken arms or bony legs, they just wanted to get him home to love. They believed they had enough love to make everything all right for both of us. One brother and one sister, we would become a happy family.

From the beginning, he was my dear brother. I called him Yaya and he called me Sasha. When we were little, people often thought we were twins – his birthday is June 21 and mine is June 23, so you can see in many ways we are connected in this big wide world.

From my brother, I have learned that two things can be true at the same time. I love my brother and will always love him, but sometimes, I get so angry with him. His world revolves around me and our family, where as my world is creative and expanding. I love being who I am. Mom says I have a strong sense of self. I live my life for a purpose.

On the other hand, Iyal's life is centered around me so much that if he could breathe my very air I think he would! His needs are overwhelming and lots of time I feel smothered. Sometimes I think every member of our family gets smothered by Iyal's needs, which are so great you could never fill his empty bucket of lost love and care.

Iyal's birth mother was a very young woman of Tartar descent and his father, Azerbaijani. She probably felt very alone when she made an adoption plan for her little baby boy to go to the Children's House.

Chapter One

MFB

MY FANTASTIC BROTHER

When my brother Iyal was in his birth mother's **womb**, she drank alcohol. When someone is going to have a baby, and drinks alcohol or takes certain pills or smokes cigarettes, it hurts the baby growing inside. My big brother was hurt forever because the alcohol damaged his brain before he was even born. He is affected by this every single day of his life. It makes me sad because I know that he has to work really hard every moment to be easy to live with.

Babies, whose birth mothers drink alcohol, can

develop **fetal alcohol spectrum disorders (FASD)**. There are many disabilities included in **FASD**. Alcohol affects the brains of these babies and prevents them from doing some things. It also affects their bodies. My brother has brain injury from alcohol that arrived in his body when he was in the womb of his birth mother. We don't think she knew this would hurt her baby.

 I often need to explain to my friends that Iyal cries a lot and is very sensitive. Because he has FASDs, he can't always control his feelings or his actions. My friends accept this explanation, which makes me feel a lot better when he has a reaction. I know it's not his fault, and it makes me feel selfish, but sometimes I just want to be a regular eleven-year-old girl. It's very hard having a brother who teases, babbles about nothing, and gets on your very last nerve! It is very hard to remember

that this is just HOW my brother IS!

 It really is not his fault. His life is full of struggles. He always has to work so hard not to fall apart, to behave. I have to remind myself that he is not always in control of what he says and does. He isn't annoying me on purpose.

Every now and then

I want to scream –

because he teases me so badly

especially when

we are out in public!

Try to imagine how hard it is to live with someone this way, someone with FASDs. Someone who teases you and babbles your name in sentences almost all the time. It is so annoying.

When he is thinking about me, my name just pops out of his mouth.

Moraaaaaaaaasha and

Morashaaaaaaaaaaaaaaaa!

My name goes in and out, around and around, louder and softer. He sings songs with my name, instead of the right words. This drives me crazy! When I am trying to think or study and he says my name, it is like a volcano in my world explodes.

You see, when someone says my name I listen. That is the problem – it is a big inter-RUPTION!

Is he talking to me?
Is he talking about me?
Is he happy with me?
Is he mad at me?

Inside I am screaming
Would he JUST shut up!

It goes on all the time.
JUST IMAGINE.

But deep inside

I love him so much!

Chapter Two

A SAD DISCOVERY

By the time my brother and I were around three years old, my parents started to notice that something was going on with him. They took him to a special kind of doctor and they found out that my brother has FASD.

I didn't really notice anything. He was just my brother, and though he was bigger than me in size, we always played together. We liked playing with our toys and we were really good friends. We liked playing outside in our toy car. My mom would pull the front and he always pushed the back. Because he was able to walk before me I always got to ride. Iyal was always really strong and he gives BIG hugs. Sometimes they hurt because he doesn't always know how to be gentle. He tries, but he forgets.

When we were little we played together and we would go to the swimming pool. Iyal has always been a really good swimmer. We learned when we were only three or four. We loved playing in the water together. Our Pop-pop (our nickname for my mom's father) taught us to swim. He used to teach swimming to high school kids. He's a really awesome teacher and he works at a kids camp in the summer, Camp Riverbend. He has taught thousands of kids to swim for over fifty years! He teaches with FUN! For the freestyle we would scoop ice cream out of an invisible tub to move our arms correctly and for kicking we all got to splash Pop-pop in the face and he laughed.

Pop-pop and Giggy (that's my mom's mother) came to visit us a lot when we were little. They actually were waiting at the airport when we first arrived in the United States. Pop-pop and Giggy stayed with us for the first six weeks we lived in our new house.

Giggy was an artist. She taught us how to paint and bought us easels. They were both teachers and believed strongly in teaching new things to children. They could see something was not quite the same for Iyal when he was trying so hard to learn new things. Pop-pop and Giggy used their imaginations to teach Iyal lots of stuff.

It was really sad when Giggy died because she and I would play dolls together. It was like she was waiting to be a grandma her entire life and was blessed with me and Iyal. I was only five when she died and it doesn't seem fair.

I miss her hugs and being together. I miss Giggy like I miss Iyal being able to have all the opportunities in life that I have. It is kind of the same feeling. My heart hurts really way down deep inside.

When I found out my brother was going to have a hard life because of his brain injury, I really didn't get it at first. I didn't do anything differently. As I got older, and my mom and I talked about it more, I began to understand. I guess she kind of knew when to teach me more about disabilities because things began to make sense.

Even now, I can't totally understand all the stuff the brain is in charge of . . .

but I see how when

a brain doesn't work the right way . . .

a lot can go very wrong.

Chapter Three

OUR FAMILY

The special doctor told my parents that Iyal has a certain kind of brain damage. Organic brain damage – this means he had the injury at birth. It didn't happen after he was born. Because Iyal's birth mother drank alcohol when he was inside of her, he has a lot of pieces that have been interrupted or changed from who he could have been. As you know my brother, Iyal, has some trouble, and it is very hard to live with.

I say to my brother "I love you," but it is like his brain does not always connect to my words. My parents think that my brother is unsure of himself. He seems to need a lot of reassurance. I think so too. He's always saying to us,

"You don't love me!" or

"You don't like me!"

Sometimes, he screams,

"You hate me."

Then he cries.

My mom says this has something to do with "attachment" — which has to do with feeling loved and safe and it begins when you are a very small person.

Lately, he'll ask these questions anywhere and everywhere. He won't care where it is, he just wants to make sure we love him. He even asks me on the bus coming home from school when I'm in front of all/some/or one of my friend(s). It is so embarrassing. Of course I LOVE HIM, but I don't want to say that aloud at that very moment, in that very place, in front of my friends. But, I know if I don't, he will get upset. And when Iyal gets upset, he will cry or throw a fit and life can be very hard. His behavior doesn't scare me, but it makes me feel two things at one time. I want my brother to be happy, but I also want to be happy and have fun.

> Sometimes he gets right in the middle,
> and my heart
> and mind pull on both sides.
>
> When I explain to my friends
> why he does that,
> they say "aww that's sad" or "awww."
> I reply, "Yes, it is sad."

There are many levels of **fetal alcohol spectrum disorders (FASD)**. Some people with FASD have many problems and other people have less, but any kind of alcohol-related disorder presents some kind of challenge.

- It is a mental health problem and can cause unusual behavior.
  Iyal has a very hard time handling his feelings.
- It can be an intelligence problem and affect how a person learns.
  Iyal has a very hard time learning new things.

- It can be a memory problem and affect remembering.
  Iyal forgets things easily.
- It can be a physical problem and affect a baby's heart, or face, or other parts of the body.
  For Iyal, all of his injury and damage is hidden until you spend time with him.
- It can also affect the way a person hears, sees, smells or feels things.
  For Iyal, it is difficult to know where his personal space is and he always jumps into my space bubble.

This has led to the creation of "My Invisible World" because people don't see what I really live with.

Some moments are very good
and some are really bad.

Chapter Four

LIFE LONGGGGGGGG

FASD is a lifelong disability. That's like forever! Once it happens, you can't take it back. up to **1 out of 100 babies have FASDs!***

That's **A LOT** of babies and no one knows exactly how many in the tens of thousands.

- It means in the United States at least **tens of thousands** of babies are born every year with this disability.
- And it means **tens of thousands** of babies will have trouble living a happy and successful life.

*Source: www.nofas.org

* They will struggle in school
  and people will not understand
  why they have behaviors
  that don't seem to make sense.

* Or why they look like a teenager
  but act like a kid in fourth grade.

- It also means **tens of thousands** of babies will have BRAIN INJURY that **could have been prevented!**

- **Tens of thousands** of babies each year . . .
  double that in two years . . .
  triple the number in three years . . .

WHEN WILL IT STOP!!!!!

Not soon enough as far as I am concerned.

FASD is an easy thing to stop. But it seems that some people don't even know about it. That floors me because every day our family is flavored with FASD-isms. And I don't always like the flavor.

All moms need to do
    when they are pregnant . . .
        going to have a baby . . .
is NOT DRINK ALCOHOL.

Even though he says he isn't, I think my brother is mad at his birth mother, but he says he's not. I know that my brother has FASD. It hurts my heart to know that my brother has a brain injury that no one in my family could help to prevent.

Every now and then he asks my mom, "Why was I born with a boo-boo on my brain?"

I feel so bad.

"How come my birth mom drank alcohol when I was in her tummy?"

My tummy answers by twisting into a knot.

When I was little my mother told me that Iyal had a disability and I kept that in mind. As I get older, it's starting to get harder and harder. My life is very creative and fun. Also, I love thinking of new ideas and I like to read my favorite book series. I enjoy talking with my friends about things I like or going to new places and exploring new things. In a way, I have left Iyal behind. My brain keeps growing and changing and loving new things. I dream of going to middle school and high school and college. I see this all as a very exciting adventure. It will be very cool.

Iyal's brain grows much slower. It's like pieces of his brain were never even built because the alcohol killed some of his brain cells. There are just spaces and empty places where important connecting parts should be.

It's sort of like when you're just about to finish putting together a really great puzzle that you may have worked on every day for a whole week. And when you get to the last five pieces you realize they're probably lying underneath some old toy that has become the bottom of a rickety tower of toys that is hiding behind the closet door in the den. It's too late to try and find them because you're absolutely, positively, done with your incredible creation.

You have to move on.

And that makes learning new things frustrating. When Iyal comes to something he has never done before, he gets nervous.

He may tantrum,

    or even rage –

    which is worse than a tantrum.

Mom explains that a rage is like a chemical storm inside Iyal's brain and we have to wait for it to pass before he can really "hear" what we are saying. Usually, when Iyal begins to calm down, he starts to cry. And then he whispers, "Sorry Mom."

This is the part

    that really gets to me.

My brother likes to keep things the same so he can feel safe. My parents say that things need to be predictable all the time. Sometimes this can get extremely boring.

Usually, he likes friends who are younger than he is. I guess I can understand that part. Even though Iyal is "growing up" physically, his brain is standing still. This difference was not such a big deal when we were little.

I feel sad leaving him behind now, though. At the same time, being able to deal with him can be so frustrating. I didn't know that it was going to be this tough. I realize now that no matter how young or old we are it's always going to be hard for Iyal. Much harder than for me.

Chapter Five

GRAND SLAM OR SHUT OUT!

It seems you never know who or what is going to come into your life. Something might go right past you OR hit you right in the face. Disabilities seem to hit you in the face, they don't fly right by. As a matter of fact, they can hit you so hard – it's like they become a part of you. But in a way, they are just a PART of you – not the whole you.

In my case, life is like a baseball game. Sometimes you might hit the ball so high that it touches the sky. You forget about it, like a phase you go through quickly. Sometimes you try to bunt it and it's a strike! That was the last strike of the game and your team loses. Everyone is mad about it, and you don't forget for a long time.

It's like something you said that hurt your best friend's feelings. They'll forgive you, but sometimes you can't forgive yourself.

When you are playing a game you have to pay attention. Iyal has a very difficult time paying attention unless he is playing his video game, then it's best not to bother him. On the other hand, if he WANTS attention he is like a big baseball mitt. All the attention goes directly to him and everyone tries to catch his ball and hold on. In fact, he gets so much attention that there are times I feel like no one even realizes I am there. This is when my invisible world gets really BIG and I feel really small.

When my brother comes home from school, his brain is tired. He has put so much energy into being good and trying his best that all his bottled up feelings come pouring out. It can be really hard for everyone and the worst part is I get lost in his struggles. Sometimes it takes until bedtime to tell Mom about my day.

Home runs for the other team ARE permanent and you can't take them back. Can you? You can't re-run them. A baby fed alcohol in a mommy's tummy can't cough it up. There is never a do-over, the baby's game was lost before they even got a chance to bat. The full potential of a life is forfeited.

Chapter Six

SECOND CHANCES

Mom and Dad decided to give two kids a second chance and they went all the way to Russia to get me and Iyal. Then when Iyal was ten, Mom decided Iyal needed a service dog to help him. Service dogs cost lots of money and need special training to do their jobs.

We didn't know if anyone had ever trained a service dog for a boy with FASD. Then, we found a place called 4 Paws for Ability, and they were willing to try. They had just the dog for my brother. His name is Chancer, a big, loveable Golden Retriever.

The service dog training program began training him hoping to find him a family and child that he could help. We found out that Chancer lost his first home, Iyal and I lost our first home, too. All of us are second chancers.

4 Paws for Ability believes the love, companionship and independence a service dog provides should be available to everyone with a disability. 4 Paws is one of the few agencies in the United States to work with very young children. It is the only agency existing in our country which has been placing service dogs with children who have Autism for 10 years. They also place Seizure Alert Dogs and dogs for medically fragile children. FASD was just a next step and we were the family!

Iyal got Chancer in February of 2008 when Iyal and I were in the fourth grade. Pop-pop helped us get him and even came to our twelve-day training. It was Chancer's second chance and our family's second chance to grow stronger.

Mom, Iyal, Pop-pop and I traveled to Ohio to get Chancer. My cousin met us there. We stayed in a great hotel with a kitchen and two bedrooms and the very first night Chancer got to come "home" with us!

When we first saw Chancer he was in his crate in this huge room. We could not wait to hug and kiss him. All the families saw all the dogs at the same time and it was crazy. But a cool kind of crazy. Noise, romping, licks and the smell of moving dogs. People were laughing and talking and dogs were barking. Everyone was excited and full of hope.

Chancer liked our family right away. He knew from the minute he met Iyal, this was HIS boy. I really don't understand how a dog can know these things – but apparently they know way more than some people do.

Chancer was happy.
    His brown eyes sent signals of dog happiness.
        He was OUR dog,
            okay, he was really Iyal's dog.
    I was really glad at *that* moment
        that I was Iyal's sister.

Chancer is Iyal's service dog. He is a BIG help and can also be BIG trouble. After all, he is a dog! And Iyal is a brother! Chancer helps Iyal calm down by laying on top of him or nuzzling him. Chancer has a really big smile and deep wise eyes. He looks like he knows a lot. His tail can wag so hard he can almost knock you over.

    When we first got Chancer, Iyal wasn't as attached to him as he is now. Now, Iyal goes up and gives hugs and kisses to Chancer. Chancer usually kisses him back. All over his face and especially his ears. Which, in a way, might not be such a bad thing. They could probably use a cleaning every now and then! Even though it's cute, his licking can get out of hand sometimes like when Iyal has his mouth open. That's really gross. But Iyal is a boy, after all, and Chancer is a dog. They actually go pretty well together. And that is the whole idea.

Chapter Seven

"TALK TO THE PAW"

When a dog is going to be a trained service dog they have to behave like a service dog. There are a lot of steps to being a service dog. First, the dog has to be chosen by the training agency and have a very good, calm temper. My brother has an enormous amount of energy all by himself. He could be his own power plant!

This is the cool part. Chancer is the calm one. He calms everyone down, especially my brother.

When my brother is calmer, it is easier for everyone else to be quieter, too.

Second, the dog has to go to a prison to be trained in obedience by inmates for many weeks. Chancer lived with two women when he was in the prison. They had a group training session every afternoon. Dogs chosen by 4 Paws for Ability learn basic commands like sit, come, down, heel, free and many other things. Everyone wins when they train the dogs. The people in prison get a big furry dog to love and teach and they learn about obedience and discipline right along with the dogs. I am sure it is happy and sad when the dog gets to join their new family. The new family is really happy, but the people in prison will miss their furry students.

Then, the dog goes back to 4 Paws for Ability. Next, it's sent to a foster home where it gets special training for the new family. 4 Paws has all its families make a video of the child who is receiving the service dog. They actually tell the family what kind of situations they want to see – like going to the store, playing outside, or eating dinner. Since my dad is a rabbi, we spend a lot of time at our temple.

So we needed to make sure that Chancer would be comfortable in our sanctury. At least he gets to sleep during Dad's sermons!

4 Paws wanted to see a normal, daily routine with stuff like that. Mom made a video of our family and Iyal's different behaviors. The dog trainers watch the video to get ideas for dog commands to help our family.

For example, "NUZZLE", is a command we give to Chancer when Iyal needs affection to help him feel better. Another important command is "OVER". For Chancer, that means he lays on Iyal when Iyal is really "active." Because Chancer is so big, the pressure he puts on Iyal helps him settle down.

Months go by and the dog gets to bond with and learn from the foster family. A dog's foster family teaches dogs how to get along well with humans. The dog works with the trainer to get really good at certain behaviors and new tricks. These tricks will have voice and hand signals that the dog likes to obey. 4 Paws dogs are trained with positive training, that means no one ever hurts the dog when they are teaching it new things. Dogs trained with positive learning like to think and do all kinds of behaviors.

When they are ready, they get to go to meet their new family. That's where we came in. We went to Ohio for 'people training' every day for twelve days. At the end of the training, Chancer and Mom had to take a test in order to become legal. When the dog and the handler pass the test, they become certified or official under the rules of the United States government.

Once the team is certified, the dog can finally go home with it's family. I could tell that Mom was really relieved after the test was over. She doesn't like to take tests. I guess I can understand that part.

Chapter Eight

JUMPING IN WITH FOUR PAWS

This was really weird. We didn't realize just how big Chancer was when he was at the 4 Paws training center, but we sure figured it out when we got back to the hotel.

Everything looked small compared to Chancer!

When Chancer layed down on the bed, he took up almost the WHOLE bed. And then he flipped around and made a mess of the covers and sheets.

Chancer's feet looked like bear's paws. They were huge! And they made this silly sound when he walked on the kitchen floor in the hotel room – kind of a swishing sound. I guess it was a combination of his fur and his toe nails.

At least we would always know where he was.

Plus, he sure was busy!

See…the hotel was a new experience for him. There were new smells, sounds and people compared to the training center. My mom's cousin, Adair, flew all the way from Montana to Ohio to help with Chancer's training. Well, she was there to help take care of Iyal and me. But I think she was also there to help take care of mom…who really needed another adult to help her out with all of this training business. Mom grew up with cats. Chancer was going to be her very first dog. Ever!

So, the first night that we had Chancer with us at the hotel, Adair took him for a walk outside. My mom did stuff in the hotel room and Pop-pop took Iyal and me for a swim in the hotel's indoor swimming pool.

We were in Ohio in January and it was really

cold outside. The hotel pool was freezing, but there was also a hot tub that Iyal and I used to get warm. We were actually having a nice quiet time together. That, unfortunately, doesn't happen much of the time. Warm and cozy makes things better for Iyal.

Then, all of a sudden, my cousin came in to the pool area and said, "Hey it's time to go!" Iyal and I knew she meant we had to get out of the hot tub.

But Chancer didn't.

"Go" meant "go"!

Well, most dogs love water. Right?

We learned right then that Chancer LOVES water. I guess he saw us . . . or saw Iyal, "his boy".

He pulled the leash so hard, my cousin let go. With an Olympic leap - Chancer jumped right into the hot tub! It was like a big furry dog cannon ball and hot water went everywhere!

It was hilarious!

I couldn't blame him.

It did feel great.

I knew right then that Chancer was going to be a fur-ever perfect brother for Iyal. I mean, Chancer had just met Iyal that day. Somehow he knew he was supposed to be looking out for Iyal. I still don't understand how Chancer knew this after **only** one day!

I thought this was very cool because I realized that Chancer could help Mom sometimes with one of her troubles. Iyal would just run out into the street without looking. Chancer would be able to help with that!

It seemed like

they BOTH needed each other.

So, at first, Iyal was tethered to Chancer. That means that Iyal wore a special vest (like Chancer did when he was working) with hooks that attached them to each other. Mom had a leash that was attached to Chancer. The three of them were all attached to each other! We practiced by going for walks or shopping at the store. It sounds like they looked like a big spider or something – but it really didn't look like that. Iyal could walk with all of us just like everyone else walks with their families. After just a few months we no longer needed the tether. Iyal did not seem to dart out into the street as much as he used to.

In some ways, Iyal has also learned to be more loving to all of his family. He certainly knows that Chancer is "his boy" and loves to get licks and kisses from his dog. And Chancer is really patient with Iyal and that has made a huge difference for Iyal.

Chapter Nine

AN unAMUSEMENT PARK

For as long as I can remember, my family has visited Pop-pop. We go to his best friend's summer camp that is designed for children to have fun and learn new things. That is where Pop-pop is a swimming teacher and also the grandfather of the camp.

We went to New Jersey the first summer that we had Chancer. My friend, Gabby, and I had a sleepover at Pop-pop's house. We went to this place where Iyal and I had gone before when we were younger and loved it! It was an outdoor amusement park where you went on rides and had a lot of fun. Gabby and I wanted to bring Chancer and Mom said we could.

While we went on our very FIRST ride, an employee of the amusement park came up to my mom and said firmly, "Dogs are not allowed here." Of course my mother gently replied, "I'm sorry, but this dog is a service dog and it would be against the law to kick us out." Well, my mom probably said it even nicer than that. She usually chooses her words very carefully.

The man went to find his manager. By that time we were done with our ride so we went to stand by Mom and Chancer. Iyal was not with us because he was at his sleep-away camp and sometimes even a dog needs time away from Iyal.

The manager was looking at Chancer and talking with my mom. Then all of a sudden he said, "I'm sorry, but you can't stay here. It's Saturday and we're really busy here tonight. If it were a different night . . ." I looked at him like he was an alien or something. Then he said, "People are telling me that their children are afraid of the dog."

I'm thinking to myself, "First of all Bozo, we're outside and people can go where ever they want and you have plenty of space. No one's telling you to stand 20 feet away from the Ferris wheel or two feet in front of this dog!"

How could anyone be afraid of Chancer?

He is a very mellow fellow. Chancer smiled, because he always smiles. Mom, however, did not smile. I could tell that my mom was probably saying bad words to herself – since she couldn't say them aloud to the man without being arrested or something. I knew from the way her body was very still that she was furious. It's what I imagine a volcano would be like – a minute before it blows its top.

She explained **again** to "the guy" that this dog was an Assistance Dog and it would be violating the **ADA Act** to make us leave. I do not think he replied.

My mother didn't want to make a big deal about it, "Sorry girls." While we were going, I glared at him as if he had nineteen ears and horns to match. Chancer just wagged his tail and smiled. Chancer always smiles.

After this event, we went to a restaurant and the people there were really glad to see us! Our waitress actually got down on the floor near Chancer to talk to him. She told us that all the other waiters in the restaurant were jealous that we sat in her section, not theirs! I thought this was funny. Especially since these people seemed really glad we were there.

I whispered, "I'm sorry that happened and we had to leave," but Gabby said it was fine. She is a good friend. Life is like that in my invisible world. You never know when the rug is pulled out from under a fun time because people don't understand.

I could tell my mom was sad (I think) because she wanted to make up for having to leave the amusement park. So we went out for ice cream and even got ice cream sundaes. After that we went back to Pop-pop's house and caught fireflies. We put them in jars to watch them glow and then we let them go – flying free and away and happy. We went to bed and Chancer slept with Mom.

When I look at Chancer sleeping, or I see Mom sleeping with our big, furry, dog, I know he came to our house to keep us peaceful and loving. He is our family's angel. He just happens to be a dog.

Mom wrote a letter to the editor of a big newspaper about what happened at the park. It was published which made us feel better. Mom's says this is called "advocacy" which I will tell you more about in the next chapter.

Chapter Ten

I LOVE MY MOM, but . . .

I don't know about you, but sometimes I have both good and bad feelings about someone at the very same time. It's like this, there are days when I am so proud of my mom (and my dad) for spending so much time doing things to make Iyal's life easier. Sometimes, though, I just wonder what it would be like if things were different. Sometimes I just wish my parents weren't so BUSY!

    They go to meetings.
        And then they go to more meetings.
    They talk on the phone to people.
        And then they talk with more people.
    They write letters.

They write email
They send faxes.

Then they talk on the phone some more!
Sometimes they travel to other states
    and even other countries.

__Mom says this is called "advocacy."__
Advocacy is when you care a lot about an idea, a person, a group of people or a place – and your voice becomes very important.

When you advocate for someone,
    you stand up for them.
    You help them get what they need.
Because sometimes their voices
    can't be heard
        – for a whole bunch of reasons.

So this advocacy thing is really important for people with special needs. Especially kids! After all, they're just kids. Let's face it, kids don't always get the attention they deserve. Mom's taught me that, for Iyal, it's especially important that he can talk about his disability and feel okay about it. Because FASDs are "invisible" or mostly hidden, people usually jump to conclusions when they see Iyal "misbehaving." And that's where Iyal needs to learn that it's okay to talk about having a disability or a brain injury.

Mom worries all the time about Iyal winding up in the wrong place at the wrong time because he likes to please people so much. Making friends means a lot to Iyal. It would be so easy for him to wander off with a stranger. Iyal also always wants to give kids his stuff, too.

>>His toys,

>>>his Pokeman cards.

>>>>**Money!**

I think you can see where this is going.

Since Iyal doesn't understand that once you give these things away you usually don't get them back…it creates big problems down the road. That's another issue. Iyal takes things literally. So, if you say the words…he won't get it if there's an underlying message. He doesn't understand when something is an "expression". Like if you say, "Hit the road" but you mean "Get going" or "It was a piece of cake" for "That was easy". Iyal might think about slapping the road or eating cake and that's the literal meaning of the words.

One time I was having dinner with Iyal and I exclaimed, "Iyal, you haven't even touched your food!" So, first Iyal "touched" the food on my plate with his finger (gross) and then he "touched" his own food. I sat there looking at him. Speechless! Then I looked at Mom and she smiled.

So these are the kind of things that my mom and dad are always watchful for with Iyal. I guess they feel pretty protective of him. They worry about people taking advantage of him . . . because he looks a lot older than he thinks or feels. While I worry about Iyal, too . . .

I also worry about me.

What if kids have never heard of FASD and think I'm making this up or think that I have this disability too?

Will I always be known as the girl whose brother has that brain thing?

I don't want to be mean or anything…but there are days when I want to be known for who I am, not because I'm the sister of that boy with special needs. I guess the really hard part is that deep inside I just feel sad.

It's really hard when Iyal is crying and says, "I'm a bad boy. Why can't I do things like Morasha?"

So, even when I feel like I live on the continent of "Iyal" – and the country of "Morasha" hasn't been discovered yet – I remind myself that there must be a reason we were all brought together as a family. Even though I sometimes say, "It's not fair" when Iyal always gets to sit wherever he wants in the van or when we can't ever change our plans last minute because Iyal will be upset – I know that this advocacy thing is more important than who sits where.

No one in my family can fix Iyal's brain problem. There is no cure for people who are exposed to alcohol when they are babies inside their mother's womb. All we can do is try and support Iyal and help him feel good about himself. We work hard to focus on his strengths and abilities. It makes a difference when he feels successful. My whole family tries to help Iyal understand that we care about him no matter what.

Mom and Dad also work to help me understand. Some days it is a struggle. We all must be kind and patient to help Iyal be his best. It sure is a good thing that moms and dads have been around longer to see the "bigger life picture".

It is harder for us kids to do that.

Chapter Eleven

OUT AND ABOUT

When my mother and I go out shopping with Chancer I usually get asked "What's the matter?" People automatically think something is wrong with me. They just can't get it into their head that it's okay for people to all be different. Some people need to wear glasses or use a wheelchair for better abilities. I reply, "Nothing, the service dog is for my brother, but we just wanted to take him for a walk. My brother is not here right now." The person who asks that question responds "Oh," or nothing at all and turns away.

I get that a lot.

It's quite annoying.

When we walk past people who have little kids they say

"Look that's a working doggy."

Or

"No-don't pet the doggy its working"

Or

"You have to ask if you can pet the doggy."

Kids usually are friendly and curious so they ask to see and pet Chancer. If we're not in a hurry my mom says "Sure." Some adults (which is kind of rude) just come right up and pet Chancer. When people do that Chancer looks at them funny, as if to say, "Can't you see I am working, did you leave your manners at home?"

Chancer has had to learn a lot about life in our home. We have had to learn a lot about living with a dog! **Even service dogs are not perfect and when he is not working, he is just an ordinary, playful dog.**

- He has dug holes as big as his entire head in my Dad's nice grass.
- He has chewed things he shouldn't and we had to learn that he needed things to keep busy when he was not working.
- He also is so big and strong. If he wants, he can pull my Mom around the neighborhood.

In fact, he was so stubborn when he wasn't working he had to go back to prison for retraining. We all missed him so, so much.

Mom went back to people training and this time she was serious.

No more **FREE lunch** for Chancer, **he had to grow up**.

All of us have learned to become stronger with Chancer. Iyal is more loving. My mom is more caring. My dad is funnier and probably a better rabbi and my life is a bit less invisible because with Chancer our life sticks out when we are out and about.

Chapter Twelve

VISIBLE NEW PAW PRINTS

Chancer has changed my family because he provides a calming peace for us when my brother has his challenges. Sometimes life is just too much for Iyal.

I think people often believe that my brother will grow out of FASD and "get well." That's never going to happen. Iyal will have to work hard at living his life every single day. He will still struggle with school and making and keeping friends. He will be sad because of how hard his life is. He will be mad when he sees other people able to do things he can't. FASD is a tough disability to have.

At least with Chancer, I get a chance to have a life of my own too. It is no longer "Morasha this" and "Morasha that" all the time. I hope with this book, our family and Chancer can turn on the light for FASD awareness. Together, we will keep letting people know about FASD and how hard it is to live with, but more importantly how easy it is to stop.

All moms need to do is not drink alcohol when they are pregnant . . .

    or even <u>think</u> they could be pregnant.

        There is no safe time

        or safe amount they should drink.

I hear my mom tell this to other adults all the time.

This may sound weird, but I thought all adults knew about these things. Like how adults always know how much ice to put in a glass before the soda overflows or when it's time to change the sheets on your bed. (Well it's obvious if you ate Oreo cookies in your bed.) It seems like an easy decision to make if you know the facts.

If anyone doesn't believe that drinking alcohol could hurt your baby before it's born . . . they should come live with us for a few days. But that's like telling someone to wear a blindfold for a few days or put really good ear plugs in their ears. Hmmm. Maybe that's not such a bad idea. It would give all human beings a chance to "see" what it's like being blind or imagine not being able to hear very well. I suppose it would help us understand how different it can be to live in someone else's world.

If you know someone who has FASD, it can be really lonely for that person and it would be really kind for good people to reach out. Meanwhile, the Winokurs try really hard to make the best of living as a family with a person who has FASD. We enjoy each other and have fun even on some of the really hard days. Luckily, Chancer enjoys EVERY DAY and we laugh. Chancer came to our home and into our hearts to make us laugh.

He is so funny when he romps around with his yucky bone in his mouth pretending we can't get it from him. He can act so goofy around the house when he's allowed to be "just a dog." But you really have to respect him when he's out working in his red vest. He listens way better than most kids I know.

My middle name is Rael, which means guardian. Chancer can have that title now, because that is exactly what he does. He is like the guardian dog angel. If Mom needs me, I'm happy to serve as the assistant dog handler. All of us love Chancer because Chancer loves us!

Paws Up and High Five!
Morasha

GLOSSARY

ADA ACT –	America Disabilities Act, 1990
Azerbaijan –	A country on the Caspian Sea between Russia and Iran.
FASD –	Fetal Alcohol Spectrum Disorders.
Service dog –	A dog certified to help people.
Tartar –	A minority people in Russia.
Womb –	Area in the female body where a baby grows.

QUESTIONS

1. What is Morasha's brother's disability? (page 12)

2. About how many babies are born in the United States with this disability each year? (page 23)

3. How do children get this disability? (page 11)

4. Can it be prevented? (page 24)

5. How can it be prevented? (page 25)

6. Can you get well from this disability? (page 54, 59)

7. What did Morasha's brother get to help him? (page 32)

8. What can young people do to help a person living with this disability? (look in my scrapbook - it's there!)

Do you want to know more?
Visit these websites:

Service Dogs
www.4PawsForAbility.org

Fetal Alcohol Spectrum Disorder
www.TheChancerChronicles.com
www.BetterEndings.org

National Organization on Fetal Alcohol Syndrome
www.nofas.org

Centers for Disease Control
www.cdc.gov/ncbddd/fas

Elementary
Early Reader

Chancer is on FaceBook
and he has NEW BOOK!

Nuzzle - Love Between a Boy and His Dog

another good book is
The Best I Can Be - Living with Fetal Alcohol Syndrome or Effects

Middle School
High School

This was written by 13-year old Liz Kulp who lives everyday with the challenges of living with FASDs.

Morasha's
Scrapbook

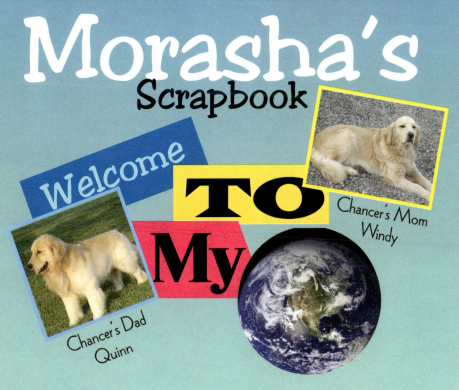

Welcome TO My

Chancer's Mom Windy

Chancer's Dad Quinn

Our adoption announcement.

We are proud to announce the adoption
of our daughter

Morasha Rael
מורשה ראל
born June 23, 1998

and our son

Iyal Navon
א׳ל נבון
born June 21, 1998

Donnie and Harvey Winokur

I have to admit, the hat DOES look ridiculous! I sure look cute, though! The day after my adoption – Mom and I are ready to explore Moscow! Two days after we were brother and sister – Iyal already wants me to wake up and play with him!

At eighteen months, I was "telling my story" in pictures.

Oh, the days we spent rocking in our favorite chairs.

Iyal and our Pop-pop have a very special relationship.

My beloved "Giggy" shares books with me.

And fun with Aunt Joyce and Uncle Jed (my mom's brother).

We actually shared . . . when we were little.

I LOVED my cupcake!

At five, I wanted to be a rock star and Iyal liked Clifford, the Big Red Dog. We think Chancer is a lot like Clifford.

Red is a good color for me ... it is a "power" color.

When you're four years old, you always want what your sister has - even if it's the same toy.

It's fun being a kid!!

I wanted to 'text' . . . even at two years old!

First day of Kindergarten.

Here I am dressing up like my dad when he goes to work. He's a rabbi. And he works a lot!

Iyal and I visited the Great Swamp in New Jersey.

We were quite the pair and ready for some Halloween treats!!

And we didn't even know how badly we needed him!

A litter of pups at 4 Paws for Ability.

Itsy Bitsy Chancer.
It's hard to imagine HE was
ever THIS TINY!

4 PAWS for ABILITY TRAINING

Mom and I worked hard to practice "tethering" with Chancer.

We spent a lot of time training.

This is what love looks like. See what I mean by being the best dog for Iyal?!

We even had a training exercise at the mall!.

Chancer and his friend Dante.

We taught him how to "high five".

Mom and Chancer getting ready to take the service dog test with lead trainer, Jeremy.

Pop-pop getting to know Chancer in our training class. Mom and Chancer at 4 Paws for Ability.

My good friend, Belle, and me at the beach.

What would a girl do without her BFFs?

We had fun at Iyal's summer camp!

Chancer on a play date with his BFF - Lucky.

FRIENDS

FAMILY

Mom, Iyal, and me.

Dad, Chancer, and Eilat tucking in Iyal.

Manhatten sleeps with me every night and Chancer stays with Iyal.

Manhattan supervised while I used treats to practice the "LEAVE IT" command.

My dad practicing REST with Eilat and Chancer.

We don't get to rest too often. When he has to go . . . he has to go! Rain or shine!

Iyal and Papa Doug (my dad's father) and me.

MY DAD'S FAMILY

Dad's family Aunt Ilene, Meemie, and Papa Doug.

Dad's sister, Randy and neice, Nadia with Meemie (my dad's mother), and Papa Doug.

Giggy, Pop-pop, Aunt Joyce, and Mom Uncle Jed is in the front.

MY MOM'S FAMILY

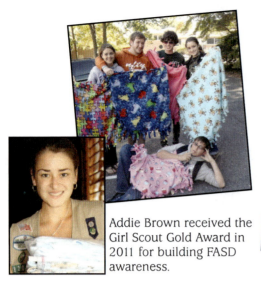

Addie Brown received the Girl Scout Gold Award in 2011 for building FASD awareness.

You can Make a Difference Blankies for Babies Project!

In 2002, my friend Liz Kulp started the Blankies for Babies program in the United States to help people know how important it is to not drink alcohol while a mom is pregnant. Children all around the world tie small fleece blankets that are given to their local clinics as first gifts for new mothers. This is a way kids can help stop this disability from happening.

You can get a little brochure for your own Blankies for Babies project at www.TheChancerChronicles.com

Then all you have to do is print out the note card and attach it to your blankets before you bring them to a clinic near you. Plus, here are some more great books about Fetal Alcohol Spectrum Disorders.

Middle School High School   Elementary Early Reader

Made in the USA
Lexington, KY
06 April 2016